COULD YOU HURRY UP THE DAWN, LORD?

COULD YOU YOU HURRY UP THE DAWN, LORD?

Poems, Prayers, and Lively
Conversations with a Loving God

JOY MORGAN DAVIS

Fleming H. Revell
A Division of Baker Book House Co
Grand Rapids, Michigan 49516

©1994 by Joy Morgan Davis

Published by Fleming H. Revell
a division of Baker Book House Company
P.O. Box 6287, Grand Rapids, MI 49516–6287

Printed in the United States of America

Library of Congress Cataloging-in-Publication Data

Davis, Joy Morgan.
    Could you hurry up the dawn, Lord? : poems, prayers, and lively con-
versations with a loving God / Joy Morgan Davis.
        p. cm.
    ISBN 0–8007–5507–3
    1. Prayers. I. Title.
BV245.D294 1994
242′.8—dc20   93–27134

For Amy Elizabeth, who was born
the same month as this book

CONTENTS

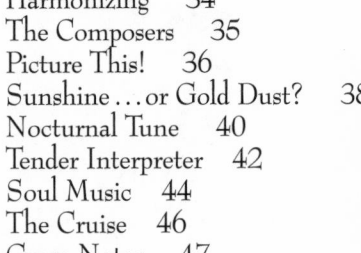

LORD, WHATEVER DRAWS ME NEARER

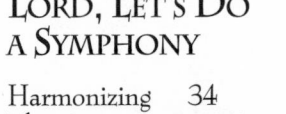

LORD, LET'S DO A SYMPHONY

LORD, STIR THE POT— IT'S BOILING OVER

LORD, MY CUP'S RUNNING OVER AGAIN

LORD, LET ME SEE YOUR DIVINE DESIGN

LORD, IT'S BEEN A LONG, LONG DAY

LORD, WHATEVER DRAWS ME NEARER

Through the Night

It's so dark,
Lord,
And my candles
Are so few . . .
Could You hurry up
The dawn?

In time, Child,
In time . . .
Dawn is never early,
But it's never late either!
Meanwhile, I've counted
Your candles . . .

Your supply is
Sufficient!

THE DAWNING

There were always things
I didn't understand,
Lord . . .
Like when some of Your
Children had so much,
And others had
So little,
When good people were
In pain or poverty,
When life was unfair
Or loss unbearable
Or strong bodies, minds,
Or hearts failed . . .
I didn't understand.

Then one day,
As I prayed for peace,
I contemplated
Your glory, Your power,
Your majesty,
Your creation,
Your cross . . .
And suddenly it
Dawned on me,
Suddenly I understood
That I don't have to
Understand!

And now I know why
You promised, "Peace
That passeth all
Understanding"!

NEARER, MY GOD, TO THEE

I wish there was
Something I could do,
Lord,
To stop the hurt . . .
It just goes on and on
Without help,
Without healing,
Without ever an
End in sight . . .
It's so hard to stay still,
To wait,
To wonder how, or if
I will endure.

I learned a long time ago,
Lord, I'd rather
Do than endure
Any day.
To do, no matter how
Difficult,
Can be exciting as you
Conquer . . .
But to endure is
Slow and sorrowful
And lonely . . .
Why must it be,
Lord?

O Child,
Surely you see,
It's the way of
The cross . . .
It's something we
Share . . .

And it lifts you up,
Toward Me.

GARDENS

Peace,
In the Garden of Eden,
Was the natural order
Of things . . .
The sun was soft,
The air was like elixir,
The lion and the lamb
Lay down together,
There was no need to
Be brave
For there was no danger,
Death, disease . . .
Peace was a natural part
Of Paradise.

But in Gethsemane
One long, lonely night
Peace was born
Only after awful anguish . . .
Only after the blood and sweat
And tears of the petition
And finally of the
Soul-surrender
Was there Peace of mind and emotion . . .
No matter the test,
No matter the danger,
Whatever the burden to bear,
Peace would be
Undaunted.

I've known both Gardens
In my time . . .
I've walked the easy paths
Of Eden
And struggled through
The thorny ways of
God's Gethsemane where
One lonely night
I reached the final soul-surrender
"Not my will, but Thine be done" . . .
And in that moment
His immortal Peace
Was *mine!*

The road returns from
Time to time
To Eden
And Gethsemane.
I've learned to welcome
Both.

One is my delight . . .
The other my
Deliverance.

MIRACLES AND MOONLIGHT

I woke just now
In the night
And found moonlight
Spread across my bed . . .
Soft, like silver silk,
A pearl-pale coverlet of
Heavenly light.

It is amazing how
Quiet I feel . . .
No qualms,
No quickened pulse . . .

Tomorrow my beloved physician,
My friend and confidant,
Will tell me the results of
The tests . . .
I wonder,
But I'm not afraid.
There have been times
I've forgotten
How much You care,
How You can turn
Tragedy into triumph
As easily as You turned
Water into wine . . .

But not tonight,
Lord . . .
Tonight I remember!

So,
I'll say
Good night now . . .
All this moonlight has made me
Sleepy.

Quiet Time

Thank You, Lord,
For this sleepless night.

I woke in the wee hours
And wandered silently
About the house . . .
Passing through the patterns
Of moonlight laid out
Across the carpet,
Warming a cup of tea
By candlelight,
Peering into the shadows
And shapes of familiar
Corners, nooks and crannies . . .
And then I sensed Your
Still small voice!
You were there
With me!

Time passed as we
Talked,
Whispering low so as
Not to waken
Sleeping loved ones,
And soon I saw the
First faint rays of dawn
As the dark began to fade.

No time now to
Return to bed, Lord . . .
We've talked
Too long.

I'm tired . . .
But happy!

Watchman, Keep My Soul

Alone in those wee hours
Between dark and dawn
The watchman keeps
His wake.
He walks with only echoes
As tho' through hollow caves . . .
While all around
The silent city sleeps,
Assured,
Since someone is awake
To sound alarms
If there is danger,
Hurt or harm,
Or thieves who threaten
To disturb the peace.

Sometimes, Lord, a night so deep
Descends upon my soul . . .
My heart seems hollow
As the silent city streets
And like a child I'm chilled
With fear . . .
The dark disturbs my peace.
Is it true, Lord,
You never sleep or slumber?

Is it true
You walk, awake,
Through the echoes in those
Deep, deserted caverns
Of the dark?

Then, dear Lord,
Until the light returns . . .
Until there's sunrise
In my soul . . .
Watch
Over me!

FRIEND OF MY FRIEND

Made in Your image, Lord,
I am so much more
Than a body and a brain . . .
I have a heart!
I can care and encourage,
I can feel.
But the difference between
You and me is
That sometimes there is
Nothing I can do . . .
To right the wrong,
To heal the broken wing,
To bind the wound,
Whereas there is *always*
Something You can do . . .
Like now,
When my friend needs help
And I am helpless.

She loves us both, Lord,
But it's You she needs now . . .

Abide with her.

THE TAILOR

I notice, Lord,
How meticulously tailored
For me
Are my problems
And my pains
So that they fit
My measurements exactly
Like a well-cut coat . . .
The burdens are never broader
Than my shoulders,
The length is never longer
Than my endurance,
The price is never more
Than I can pay . . .
Indeed, when I walk
In Your will
I see that my resources
Are always sufficient!

O, don't let me wander away!

I wouldn't want to be
Caught in a blizzard
With a coat
Too small . . .
And frostbitten fingers
You never meant for me
To suffer!

A Mystery

You would think that on
A clear day you could see
Forever . . .

But sometimes it is only
Through a veil of tears that
I can see the
Face of God.

HELP!

Well, Lord,
I've done it again . . .
Made a mess of things!
I know I've set in motion
Certain circumstances
And I'll have to
Suffer the consequences
Whether or not I'm sorry,
(Which I am)!
But could You maybe intervene
A little,
Maybe even cushion my fall?
I know it's my fault, Lord,
And I'll accept the
Repercussions . . .

I'm just asking for some
Shock absorbers!

MASTER PLAN

So well
I remember that
Long winter, Lord,
When my heart was like
A windswept field . . .
Flat, bare,
Barren . . .
When all my safe
Shelters had been leveled
To the ground.
I was open to the
Elements . . .
Stung by rains and winds
(Many of my own making) . . .
Yet wondering why
Not one shelter was
Left standing in the storm,
Why everything I'd ever
Had or held to me
Was leveled.

Then one day, in the city,
I saw an empty lot . . .
There everything had been
Torn down
Taken away
Leveled . . .

The lot prepared for the
Firm foundation
Of a new building
To be laid . . .
And then, Lord,
I knew!

On the leveled field
Of my bare life
You intended to build
A tower . . .
A structure more sturdy
Than glass or iron or steel,
So strong it could
Withstand
The flood at my feet,
So tall it could
Touch the sky . . .
And suddenly I was
Willing!
Whatever it took,
I *wanted* that
Tall tower . . .

For finally
I had recognized the
Architect!

LORD, LET'S DO A SYMPHONY

HARMONIZING

Dear Lord,
You hear so many
Heartbreaking prayers
From so many
Heartbroken people . . .
I like to think
It lifts Your spirits
To hear my thanksgiving song
This morning!
You've wept with
So many of Your children
Today . . .
Come sing with me
Awhile!

You know the music . . .
It's the song
You gave me once
In the night!

The Composers

Dear Lord . . .
Little Anna lay in my arms,
One week old and
Wonderful,
And suddenly I wanted
To sing!
No matter that I
Can't carry a tune
Or hold a note
Or harmonize . . .
There was music
In me . . .
Music!
This must be what it means
To have a
Song in my heart!

O, let's don't stop with
A song, Lord . . .
Let's do a
Symphony!

PICTURE THIS!

Dear God,
Now and then there is
A day in my life
That is perfect . . .
The sky is pure powder blue,
The grass is fresh and fine
And feels like silk
Between my toes,
I have no pain
Or problem,
And everyone I love
Loves *me* . . .
Perfect for a day
Or two or ten . . .
And I savor the sunlight!

I know the world is full of
Sorrow and suffering
And that at times
It will touch me.
I know there are disagreements
And deep regrets
That pull people apart.
I know that
Somewhere, sometime,
There will be a veiled valley
Through which we'll walk.

But today there is light . . .
So much love and sunlight
To savor . . .
And I know You intend me to!
How else would we ever see
What You meant Your
World to be,
What You created,
What You made,
Unless now and then You
Give us a glimpse . . .

Of Eden!

Sunshine . . . or Gold Dust?

Dear Lord,
It all went well
Today!

From the moment I woke
To see the sun shining through
The flying snow flurries
Until now,
While I watch the
Last light fade from
Behind the hills,
It went well . . .
My mind and body
Performed as I wanted,
My work was appreciated,
My house was a home
At peace . . .
All day!

I am thankful
For today!

But I am also thankful for
Those other days,
Those days so filled
With fault and imperfection,
For they enable me to know
Perfection
When I find it

And to treat it as a *treasure* . . .
Not just
Another day of
Sunshine!

Nocturnal Tune

My body clock is set
Somewhat behind the sun . . .
I like to sleep late,
Eat late, work late . . .
And I love
Siestas!
Six a.m. seems like
The middle of the night
To me . . .
(If I was a bird I'd
Never get any good worms).
But I'm wide awake at
Six p.m. when everyone else
Is winding down . . .
And I can see
In the dark!

Maybe that's why
Life's deep, dark hours
Don't seem so desperate
To me . . .
Many of my most
Creative times
Have happened in the night!
I see solutions then
That evade me in daylight.

Ideas and directions become
Clearer then (like stars that
Can't be seen until
The sun goes down).
And without the roar of the crowd
The "still small Voice"
Is so easy to hear!

I realize I don't
Rise and set with the sun . . .
But like the Nightingale
I'm not afraid of
The dark.

Sometimes I even
Sing!

Tender Interpreter

I used to think
The Holy Spirit pled
For me
Only when my heart
Was so heavy,
The burden so unbearable,
The agony so great,
That words were
Not enough . . .
When I could only
Weep . . .
And trust the Holy Spirit
To translate
My incoherent cries
As they rose, broken, to the
Throne of Grace.

What joy to discover
That He comes also
To my aid
In times of jubilation,
When God's goodness
Or peace or compassion
Or manifold miracles
Are so overwhelmingly
Wonderful
That there are no
Words . . .

None that are
Impressive enough
Profound enough
Large enough . . .
And I am left, literally,
Speechless!

Then,
To keep my heart
From bursting with
So many unsung psalms,
The Holy Spirit stands
Before the Throne of Grace
And translates
Into celestial languages
The exultations of
My soul's silent
Praise!

Soul Music

I passed her by,
The slender girl beside
The Kettle . . .
I was rushing, running late,
Determinedly intent upon my LIST
Of Christmas wishes . . .
But the sound of her
Silver bell had touched me
So I turned,
And threw some coins into
The Kettle.
That was the last I thought
Of it . . .
Until I slept.

At first I only heard
The bells,
Faintly, from afar . . .
But then I saw the faces,
Waiting
    Watching
        Listening also
For the bells . . .
I saw the hungry faces,
And hands reaching
For the bowls of rice.
I saw refugees from world
Wars and floods and famine
Gathered in.

I saw the city . . .
Weary children who were
Warm at last,
A man with his first full
Meal since summer,
A mother who could finally
Fill the stockings by
A meager Christmas tree . . .
And I saw more, so many more,
Comforted and cared for
With the Kettle coins!

But most amazingly . . .
Whenever one of those I saw
Was fed, or filled,
Or warmed,
More bells rang out
Joining in the jubilation . . .
Ringing, swinging, singing!
And when I woke
The joy was mine . . .
For I found the song had
Settled here
Inside me!

O,
If I had known
The coins could make
Such music in my soul . . .
I would have given
More!

THE CRUISE

Lord . . .
Is there no end
To this flood?
Your showers of blessings
Have been falling
Daily,
At least for forty days
And forty nights,
And I am floating
High, wide and handsome
In my ark
With those I love
Around me
Safe and secure . . .
I'm almost afraid to
Let my doves
Fly free . . .
I'm afraid one of them
Will find dry land,
Maybe even a
Desert
Not far away!
Can I keep them
In their comfortable cages
A little while longer?

I do so love
To cruise!

GRACE NOTES

The long silence of this
Sleepless night is
Like a vast
Empty cave or cavern
Of endless corridors and rooms,
As hollow as my
Lonely soul . . .
I shall fill it with
My whispered prayers
And listen to them echo,
Chiming softly through the chambers,
The sound waves growing
Wider, richer toned,
Till they return to me
Magnified . . .
No longer prayers,
But songs of praise!

TOGETHERNESS

Dear Lord!
I've just discovered
The most amazing
Thing . . .
Not only do I
Want to be with You,
But *You* want to be
With *me!*

That's why You
Taught us to
Pray!

LORD,
STIR THE POT—
IT'S BOILING OVER

Boiling Point

Lord,
My cauldron runneth over!
I'm in a stew
Of emotions.

How can I be so
Exhilarated
And so sad all in the
Same day?
How is it that one part
Of my life
Runs so smoothly
And another part so
Roughly?
One minute I'm communicating
With my world,
And the next minute there's
Nothing but silence . . .
Sealed lips
Closed doors
Shuttered hearts.
This morning I felt so
Beautiful, with my yellow
Chiffon floating around me
As someone said, "You never age!"

But by afternoon a harsh
West wind had made
My hair unfurl
My make-up fade
And my face look sixty,
At least!
My moods are so
Many . . .
I want to stop stewing
And simmer down!

Maybe, Lord, if *You*
Stirred the pot,
Things that are about to
Boil over
Would blend . . .
And my emotional mess
Would become a
Gourmet meal!

I'm turning
My ladle over to You,
Lord!

SWEET DREAMS

I've come, Lord,
To the clear conclusion
That my sleepless nights
Are not because I doubt
Your will . . .
(For I'm well convinced
Your will is
Always best) . . .
But it is the
Waiting, just waiting
For what You will do,
And when,
That keeps me awake
And wondering!
Can't You give me
Some idea
Of what You're
Planning?

My Child,
When the time comes
You'll know . . .
The doors will be
Wide open
And the lights
Will be on!
Meanwhile,
Of all the plans
I have for You,
Insomnia is not
One of them!

Surely Goodness and Mercy

I trusted You when
The way was dark
And the valley deep . . .

I will trust You now,
In the soft sunshine
That warms the
Still waters.

You are my
Shepherd.

LIFESAVER

Lord, forgive me
If I seem unseemly
As I hold in my hand
Your Word
Wondering where to read.
I know Your Word was
Meant not as a momentary
Anchor in an angry sea
But as a safe harbor into which
I should sail serenely . . .
Yet today I have no time
To read or pray or ponder
Except the barest, briefest
Prayer . . .
My chest is tied with ropes
Of tension,
I can't breathe,
I'll drown with these ropes
Around me . . .
Help me! Now!
In this single solitary moment
That I have,
Help me!
As a raft in a whirlpool
Lodges against a rock
And finds immediate
Stability,
Let me lodge, dear Lord,
Against Thee!

At His Feet

I can't lift it any longer,
Lord . . .
This care that is so
Heavy in my heart . . .
It consumes me,
Takes my time away from work,
Play, pleasure,
Drifts into my dreams
Disturbingly . . .
I feel I must remember
Every waking moment
How much it will mean,
The outcome and conclusion of
This care . . .
But I need rest, Lord,
I need relief!

O Child . . .
You've come so often to
My Throne of Grace
And lifted up that care
To Me . . .
This time,
When you come
Just lay it down!

A Measure of Grace

I've seen, Lord,
How You always balance
Life . . .
You never let the scales
Tip too much to
One side!
When the pressures of this
Imperfect world
Push one side down
With hardship, hurt,
Or trying times,
You place
Help, healing balm,
Strength, stamina,
And so far unseen
Solutions on
The other side!
When ashes are heaped
On one side,
You lay beauty
On the other . . .
And when loss lies heavy
One day,
You add grace and gain
The next!

So, when sometimes I feel
I've been overcharged
Or cheated
By life's hard circumstance
Help me to wait,
Patiently . . .

Till You balance
The scales!

GOD PROVIDES

I was born
Little . . .
Little hands and feet
And bones, and a back
That can't
Lift or carry or pull or push
And hurts a lot.
I cry sometimes about it,
But mostly I'm just
Tired of it . . .
Tired of being little,
Of being weak,
Of never having enough
Strength to stand in lines,
Or move my furniture
Here and there,
Or dig in the dirt of
My flowerbeds,
Or paint the porch,
Or ski.
I have to rest
When I'd rather be reading
Or shopping
Or writing my words
Or making my Asparagus Supreme.
I hate it when I have to
Stop in the middle of my day
And rest.

My husband, the man
In my life for many
Long years, has
Strong shoulders and
Arms and legs and
Love.
He finds me chairs,
Brings me refreshments,
Carries my bags,
Lifts the mattress, and
Reminds me to
Take care of his
Joy.

I wonder . . .
If I were not weak,
Would God have given him
And his strength to
Somebody else?

I'd rather have him
Than big bones
Any day.

MODERN MIRACLES

My nature just naturally
Hurries, Lord . . .
And altho' I've set aside
Plenty of time
In which to meet
My assignments
I'm breathless because
Of my mental
Fast Forward!
I'm tense
And my neck muscles are
Tied in knots
When I should be
Contemplating the pleasures
Of creativity and talent!
I love the work I'm doing . . .
It's the *way*
I sometimes do it
That worries me!

Help me remember that this
Is *not* Your will
For me . . .

Remind me that there are
More than enough hours
In each day
For work and play
And prayer and love
And lingering leisure . . .
Lead me as I select
And sort out
Which goes where . . .
Calm me with Your
Remote Control
And fine tune my
Spiritual antennas
To receive Your
Signals!

And then, Lord . . .
Send me
Your peace!

BASKETS LEFT OVER

I have only
Twenty minutes, Lord,
To tell them about You . . .
Twenty minutes is all
That is allowed for the
Lesson at the luncheon
Of busy business women
Who hurry in and hurry out,
Lunching quickly, quietly . . .
These efficient, watchful women
To whom TIME is an
Ever present companion . . .
Minutes! When it would take
Hours to feed a hungry
Soul sufficiently.

In so short a time
I can offer only
Loaves and fishes,
Like the little lad of
Galilee.
Touch it, Lord,
As You did that day . . .
And turn it into
A feast!

OUT OF SEASON

The yellow jasmine bloomed
Too soon this year . . .
It was unseasonably warm,
And they burst forth in beauty
As if their time
Had come.
But six days later
It snowed . . .
The fragile flowers froze,
Their glory gone until
Some other season . . .
Spent in just six days
Of splendor.

How like me, Lord . . .
So impatient for
The rare rewards of spring
Before winter's work
Is fully done!

Free Spirit

There was a line written
On a dungeon wall . . . "Tho' I
Cannot see the sun,
I know it's shining"!

How ashamed I am,
Lord,
That sometimes
Even in the sunlight
My heart is
Dark with doubt . . .
Sometimes I make
My own dungeons.

Help me to enlarge
My faith
    My hope
        My trust . . .

So I too can be a
Free spirit!

Waiting for Signs

Lord,
I wish I was tall enough
To see over this mountain
Rising before me . . .
There doesn't seem to be
Any way around it
Or through it
Or over it . . .
And I don't know
What's on the other
Side!

But since You obviously
Have an overview
Of the entire situation,
I'm assuming You'll
Be putting up some
Guideposts . . .

Any day now!

LORD, MY CUP'S RUNNING OVER AGAIN

LOVE'S LABOR

Just holding close the Bible that
    Once knew her tender touch,
And tracing there the verses which
    To her had meant so much,
I feel again the comfort of
    My mother's constant care,
And how her every thought of me
    Was turned into a prayer.

She knew that life was bound to bring
    Some sorrow and some rain . . .
But while she could, she shielded me
    From heartache and from pain.
She sang the well-remembered hymns,
    And read to me the Word . . .
Then lovingly she took my hand
    And led me to the Lord!

She placed my tiny hand in His
    And looked into His face . . .
"I'll tend this child of Yours, dear Lord,
    And watch her grow in grace!"
She labored in that work of love
    For fifty years, and more . . .
Until she left this earthly place
    For Heaven's golden shore!

So now she walks along beside
    The Man of Galilee,
And as they talk, she frequently
    Reminds the Lord of me!
She tells Him of my latest need,
    (As if He didn't know) . . .
And pleads with Him to help me through
    My weariness and woe!

A sweet compassion fills His face,
    As Mother takes my part . . .
Because He loved *His* mother so
    He listens with His heart!
He vows the burdens she's revealed
    Will not so heavy be . . .
And here below I feel them lift,
    For they belonged to me!

And so when paths I take are right
    Or plans are richly blest,
I know He's given honor to
    My mother's quiet requests!
Altho' she lives in other worlds
    It's clear that still she cares . . .
I live without her presence now,
    But not without her prayers!

A Psalm

The Lord is my Shepherd
    And He leadeth me . . .
Beside the still waters
    At peace I will be!
In pleasant green pastures
    My feet will find rest . . .
And there in His presence
    My heart will be blest!

My soul is restored when
    I look on His face . . .
For freely He offers
    Forgiveness and grace!
My cup runneth over
    With measures divine . . .
And daily His showers
    Of blessings are mine!

The Lord is my Shepherd
    And He leadeth me . . .
His rod and His staff for
    My comfort will be!
In goodness and mercy
    With Him I shall dwell . . .
Forever to know, "With
    My soul it is well"!

THE BEAUTY OF THE DARKNESS

O, the blessing of the burden
    That can cause a man to cry
For the hand of Someone stronger
    On Whose help he can rely.
O, the beauty of the darkness
    That can cause a heart to grope
For the light from Heaven's windows
    And refreshing rays of hope.

For it's here, within the shadow,
    That we learn to look and live . . .
And it's here, within the sorrow,
    That we sacrifice and give!
So tomorrow, on the mountain,
    We can say of days now dim . . .
"It was there, within the valley,
    That we learned to lean on Him!"

LOVE STORY

They always felt it was meant to be,
　　The way they happened to meet . . .
And when they found they had fallen in love
　　They had the whole world at their feet!
He sang and danced to the music he made
　　And vowed they would never part . . .
She laughed delighted and called her love
　　"The boy with a song in his heart!"
The candles burned in the little church
　　When they became man and wife . . .
The flames reflected the look of love,
　　For now they were linked for life!

The children came, and the circle grew,
　　When they bowed their heads to say grace . . .
And home was a harbor away from the storm
　　As they anchored their lives in that place.
They had their share of trouble and trial,
　　But gratefully counted the years . . .
Tho' sometimes the way seemed long and hard,
　　There was always more laughter than tears.
She hardly noticed when time had turned,
　　That his eyes were a little dim . . .
It mattered not that she used a cane
　　As long as she walked with him!

But then one day, at twilight time,
    When the shadows were growing deep . . .
He said good night in his loving way,
    And slipped away in his sleep.
The music stopped in her world that day,
    O how much she missed the song . . .
The days were silent without his voice,
    And the nights were all so long.
As she slept the sound of the angels' wings
    Seemed soft, and hauntingly near,
For scenes of Heaven had filled her dreams . . .
    It was home to someone so dear!

But she prayed for strength to go on with life,
    To bear the being alone . . .
And bravely she walked with a smile on her lips
    Till at last the Lord said, "Come home!"
The years fell away as she stood to go . . .
    So young she felt, and so free!
She heard then the *music* she'd missed so much,
    The same joyful melody!
Like a girl she ran to the Golden Gates,
    To love that would never depart . . .
For waiting there, with his arms open wide
    Was the boy with a song in his heart!

LORD, LET ME SEE YOUR DIVINE DESIGN

ART APPRECIATION

Lord,
Sometimes when I look
At my life
It seems like a homespun
Patch-work quilt . . .
Quaint, but not quite "together"!
There are bits and pieces of
Cloths and colors,
Scraps of material,
Tiny squares and triangles
That remind me of
The days of my life . . .
This piece from a
Dress I wore when I was
Younger, prettier,
And more petite,
That piece from a
Favorite doll,
Another from the old
Blue coat I kept until it was
Threadbare because it
Flattered my face . . .
But where's the pattern,
Lord?
Where's the plan?

When You began to put together
The days of my life
You must have known
Where each piece would go . . .
You've told me that I am
Fearfully and wonderfully
Made . . .
And I believe You, Lord,
I do!
I may not be a velvet tapestry,
But even crazy-quilts
Have purpose,
To give warmth and
Cozy comfort and
Color to a room!

Whatever I am, Lord,
You made me . . .
Lovingly,
Carefully,
Reverently,
And exactly right!

Help me to see Your
Divine design!

Sealed

I've asked You, Lord,
A hundred times . . .
Do broken hearts
Ever heal?
But You've never
Answered me . . .
You're silent on
The subject.

Perhaps it doesn't matter
If a heart mends . . .
Perhaps it only matters
If the cracks are covered over
With faith, and hope,
And a large measure
Of love.

If that's the case, Lord,
Then please cover
My heart . . .

With the greatest of these!

Because

I've been reading Your Word,
Lord, and I believe I've
Learned why it is
You bless me . . .

Not because I've earned it,
Not because I deserve it,
Not because it's due me,
But because I'm dear to You . . .
Because You love me!

No reason . . .
Just because!

WINTER WATCH

When the fire burns low
We put on another log
So it won't go out!

Why then do we neglect
Relationships that are
Burning low
Losing warmth
Dying out . . .
The spark still there,
Smoldering,
Covered in a cozy
Bed of ashes
Waiting to be fanned,
Warm, awake,
Alive again . . .
A new log of love
Or forgiveness
Or encouragement added
Until it is
Aflame,
Blue, blazing,
Beautiful once more.

Lord, help me to stack up
My logs . . .
So when winter comes
I'll be ready!

LET GO, LET GOD

I've been praying,
Lord,
Like it all depends
On You . . .
And I've been working
Like it all depends
On me . . .
I'm *trying,*
Lord!

Now help me
To *trust.*

PRAYER OF FAITH

Lord, I remember
The centurion
Who approached You
On behalf of his most
Faithful servant.
He insisted, "You need not
Come with me in Person . . .
Just speak the words
And he will be
Healed!"

You turned to him, amazed,
And You said, "I have
Never seen such
Great faith,
Not even in all Israel!"
And in that moment,
Miles away,
The man was made well!

Today, Lord,
A blessing came
Into my life . . .

A blessing
So big,
So impossibly big,
That I have been hesitant
To ask it for myself . . .
Yet, miraculously,
It is now mine!

I wonder . . .
Who approached the
Throne of Grace for me?
Who prayed for me
Today?

Whoever . . .
They must have had
Great faith!

Tongue-Tied

For me, Lord,
One of the liberating
Glories of Heaven
Will be the new language
I will learn!
The words I know now
Are so few,
So futile,
So absolutely powerless
To express
The praise I feel,
The worship, the awesome
Wonder of Your grace . . .
I'm speechless!

The disciples once requested,
"Teach us to pray, Lord!"
And so do I . . .

But first,
I'd love to learn some
New words!

SEASON'S GREETINGS

Was it, perhaps,
A mere "chance meeting,"
The girl who sat beside me
On the plane?
The tears lay on her lashes,
And I offered several
Whispered words of
Sympathy.
Was it only "a coincidence,"
The man who brought
My firewood?
His fingers were blue and
Frostbitten,
And I gave him the gloves
That were too large for
My husband's hands.
Did it "just happen,"
That I was on the
Windswept street when
A ragamuffin child appeared . . .
And wrenched my heart?
Were they only people
Passing by,
Or were they angels unawares
Sent to teach me
Tenderness?

I may have seen a
Christmas spirit!

Lavender Blue

It is twilight time . . .
A lavender sky surrounds
The lacy, lilac blooms of
The redbud tree,
While somewhere sleepy birds
Sing nightsongs
As they settle into
Their nests.
I sigh . . .
I want to turn to someone
And say, "Isn't it beautiful . . ."
But there is no one here,
And I know instinctively that
The beauty will not be as
Perfect for me as it
Might have been.

Is this why You made *us,* Lord?
Was it dusk in
The Garden of Eden?
Was the sky lavender and
The redbud in bloom?

Did You, like me,
Listen wistfully to the birds
Singing each other
To sleep?

Yes, I think it must have been
Just such a time
When You saw that nothing
Can be completely perfect . . .

Unless shared.

LIKE FATHER, LIKE CHILD

I know You've noticed,
Lord,
How I love to
Organize things . . .
Closets,
    Clothes,
        Laundry,
My life . . .
I absolutely adore
Lists!
I know what I want
To do tomorrow
And next week
And next year!
I make plans for tea
As seriously
As I make plans for
Retirement!
I want a place
For everything and everything
In its place . . .
(My husband accuses me
Of putting away
Books he's reading
Tools he's using
And shirts he's about
To put on!)
Sometimes I wonder . . .

Would I be happier if
Life was a little haphazard . . .
If some days the schedule
Got scattered and the
Loose ends never got
Tied?

O, I think not!
I feel so settled
With *order!*
I have such a sense
Of peace and purpose
Knowing when and how
And why things will be
Accomplished,
And such a pleasure in
The serenity of rest
When all is done!

Besides, I figure I
Got it from You . . .
Only an *organized* Person
Could have created the
World and all that is therein
In six days
And been through
By Sunday!

AFTER THE RAIN

Is there anything more
Spectacular than
The morning
After the rain . . .
Every blade of grass glistens,
Every leaf gleams,
The roses sparkle as if
Adorned with diamonds,
The air is clean
And clear as crystal . . .
It's a whole new world,
The morning
After the rain!

Recently it rained awhile
In *my* world, Lord.
I saw it coming,
The storm . . .
The dark clouds gathering
Around my mountain tops . . .
And like a pampered child
Wanting to go play
I pouted, "Don't let
It rain, Lord! Don't let
It ruin my day!"

But You didn't rearrange
The weather in my world,
Did You?
You didn't stop
The storm!
And now this morning
As I look at my clean, clear,
Sparkling fresh spirit
I see You were right . . .
Again!

Perhaps next time
As the dark clouds gather
I'll be wiser . . .
And more willing!

Night Visions

What is it in the wee
Small hours of the
Night, Lord,
That intrigues the mind
And touches the
Imagination?
Is it the darkness,
Where we walk with
Mystery and romance . . .
Or the stillness,
Where nothing stirs . . .
Or the solitude,
As soul and mind
And body (when not bombarded
By the noise and nuances
Of life)
Seem to blend into a
Clearer state of consciousness . . .
What is it in the
Night that lets us leave
Ourselves
For flights of fancy
Above our earthbound being?

Could it be because
In darkness
We are closer to Creation . . .
Closer to our own inherent
Creativity?

Once when there was nothing
Anywhere but darkness,
When all the world was without
Form and void,
Your imagination made
Miracles . . .
The sun, the moon,
The lion, the lamb,
The mountains and rivers and
Adam and Eve . . .
Your vision of tomorrow
Turned night
Into day!

If I'm made in Your
Image, Lord,
I'm sure to have *some*
Of Your imagination . . .
Some of the creativity
That turned ordinary atmosphere
Into a paradise!

I must remember that
Tomorrow, Lord . . .
As I make my day!

God's Business

Dear Lord,
I sometimes feel so selfish
Praying mostly about
Me and mine . . .
My plans
My husband
My children
My needs . . .
Yet all I know,
Truly know,
Is my own mind and heart.

I can see the surface
Of other lives,
But not inside . . .
I can recognize
Material needs
But not emotional ones . . .
I can weep because of
Burdens borne by someone else,
Yet not understand
Why You allow those burdens
To weigh down a spirit
Which would otherwise
Take wings.

Beyond praying
That Your will be done
In their lives,
I don't know
What else to ask.
Only *You* know
Their inmost needs . . .
Just as You know mine.

So, Lord,
I'll stay *out* of
Your business . . .
But please promise me
You'll stay *in* mine!

THE FAIR

Happiness is not a
Continuous ride on a
Carousel, sitting high
On a painted horse
With jeweled eyes and
Ribbons for reins.

Happiness is *peace* . . .
So deep it is
Undisturbed by surface
Turbulence,
And *reason* . . .
In a world that is
Unreasonable,
And *assurance* . . .
Of self, of goodness,
Of God.

And I've noticed that the
Happiest people I know
Are often those with
The most prolonged pain,
The heaviest load
To carry,
The hardest road.

Perhaps it is that they must
Depend so completely,
Keep so close to
Heaven's light
And His love
That they are never
Lost or lonely . . .

Like a child on a
Still carousel
When the music
Stops!

LEST I DASH MY FOOT

O, dear Lord!
You did it again
Today . . .
Sent Your angels to
Whisk me up
Out of harm's way!
When I think of all
The near misses in
My life,
The too-close-for-comfort
Times,
The between-the-devil-and-the-
Deep-blue-sea
Situations,
It occurs to me that
I may not have a
Guardian Angel . . .

I must surely have
Several!

LORD, IT'S BEEN A LONG, LONG DAY

ANTICIPATION

It's been another
Long, long day,
Lord.
I'm tired,
Moody, melancholy . . .

I wonder what it will
Be like,
Never to be tired,
Or sick, or sad?
I suppose
It will be just . . .

Heavenly!

Candleglow

There's one glorious
Advantage to age . . .
You no longer wait until
Tomorrow!
I wear my diamonds now
Whenever I please,
Even to picnics!
I turn on lights just
Because they make my rooms
Warm and welcoming!
I walk in the rain
Regardless of my hair!
I say "I love you"
A lot . . .
And yesterday I lit
The red candle shaped
Like a rose!
No reason . . .
Just a celebration of
Beauty!

At my age
There's no time
Like the present!

ACT YOUR AGE

It's easier to have faith
When you're fifty!
You look back on your life
And you see proof . . .
The promises He made
And kept,
The prayers He answered,
The children He protected,
The healing, the help,
His hands on your
Plans and purposes,
His timing, (which left you
Impatient and petulant), but which
Was always perfect . . .
O yes! It's easier to have faith
When you're fifty!

Then why do I so often
Act as if I'm
Twenty-five?!

Beyond Tomorrow

O Lord, she is so young,
And it's been so short a time
That she's been ill . . .
It seems just yesterday
When she was well,
Laughing, so alive . . .
And now they've said
She'll leave us soon.
It's not possible, is it?
It can't be . . .
She doesn't like the cold,
And she was never still,
She can't die . . .
Can she?

O . . .
Help me to see beyond
The door of death.
Let me look,
If only for a moment,
Into the golden city.
Let me feel the warmth,
See the light, hear the music
Of a thousand souls who sing
Of jubilee and joy.
O Lord,
Let me know a little
Of Your welcome celebration . . .

So I can bring myself
To say "Good-bye."

Sufficient unto the Day

I'm tired!

I keep taking on
Responsibilities
That are not mine . . .
The future,
Old age,
Retirement,
Tomorrow . . .
When all I really have
To make right is
Today!
The rest belongs to
Someone Else . . .
Because *I* belong to
Someone Else . . .
And according to His call
Of me, "All things will work
Together for good"!

So I will sing, "Only to be
What He wants me to be
Every moment of
Every day,"

And then all those days
Will become
Tomorrow,
Retirement,
Old age,
And I will find that
My future was His plan
All along!

Now I can rest.

VOYAGER

Lord,
I feel like that mythical
Ancient mariner,
I've been sailing life's
Sea for so long!

Sometimes it's been rough . . .
I've been storm-tossed
By wild waves of emotion,
I've been washed away on
Desert islands to languish
Until the tides of hope
Returned.
I've watched the winds
Of adversity split my sails
And splinter my mast!
But then sometimes it's been
Smooth sailing . . .
Sometimes there have been
Calm, clear,
Sunshiny days and soft
Balmy nights
And lush, lazy lagoons!

I've weathered it all, Lord.
With You on board . . .

You've been my Stabilizer,
My true Compass,
My seaworthy Companion . . .
And we seem to be straight
On course!
But I'm wondering how far
Across we've come?
Are we close to the
Other side?
Will we soon be sighting
Another shore?

It's been an adventure, Lord,
This voyage,
But I'm ready for that
Fair, final harbor . . .

Whenever!

BURIED TREASURE

In a Southern summer
The night was soft . . .
And the old house,
Settled so comfortably
Beside the country road,
Was open to the
Heavy scent of honeysuckle.
In the milky moonlight
My skin looked young again,
Pale and smooth
And silky as I sat
On the wide window seat
Listening to the silence,
Waiting, waiting,
Until the sound
Was there . . .

Faintly at first,
From far, far away
Came the whistle of the train
Crying through the night
Bringing back those things
I had thought long buried . . .
The secret tears of
Lost loves
Forgotten dreams
Accepted sorrows . . .

And soon I could not tell
My heart's cry
From the so familiar
Whistle
As it came closer,
Closer, closer,
And then went wailing
Through the distant dark.

The echo lingered
Then was lost . . .
Once more the summer night
Was silent . . .
And suddenly I understood
Why I had stayed so long
Listening!
I had been waiting for
The sound
Of my childhood . . .
Simple, safe,
Always the
Same!

But now, alas, the sound
Is gone, dissolved into
The tender night,
And I am grown again . . .
Left alone in summer's
Moonlight . . .

With my buried tears
For treasure.

FORETASTE

This morning
As sunlight streamed
Through stained glass
Windows, a beautiful
Black woman, radiant in a
Rich crimson robe,
Sang from her soul . . .
"I'm gonna' eat at
God's great welcome table
One of these days!"

I know, Lord, that I'll
Be there too,
At Your heavenly
Banquet for believers,
But I'm so spiritually
Hungry . . .
I need nourishment
Now!
Could I please have
An appetizer,
Just a foretaste
Of things to come . . .

So I can wait
Till it's time
For the feast?

19